ıotes for Personal Excellence – 1

# Relationship

One Hundred Quotes and Thoughts
with One Hundred Insightful Illustrations of Lord Ganesha

R.N. Kogata • Lalita Kogata

DK PRINTWORLD
Publishers of Indian Traditions

First Published in India, 2013
ISBN 13: 978-81-246-0713-8
ISBN 10: 81-246-0713-3



*A creation of:*
Mr R.N. Kogata and Mrs Lalita Kogata
608, Hiran Magari, Sector - 11, Udaipur, India
Phones: +91-94141 58870, +91-294-258 3870
devkush@rediffmail.com

*Printed and published by:*
D.K. Printworld (P) Ltd.
'Vedasri', F-395, Sudarshan Park
(Metro Station: Ramesh Nagar), New Delhi - 110 015
Phones: 011-2545 3975 / 2546 6019 Fax: 011-2546 5926
e-mail: indology@dkprintworld.com Web: www.dkprintworld.com

# Preface

You cannot run away from having a relationship. Be it meaningful ones, constructive ones or those that are negative. Yet, it is always our role to constantly manage these varied links and interactions. It first starts with the pondering and appreciation, and if blended with love, it gives depth to human relationships, brings people closer to each other physically and emotionally, and makes people think expansively about themselves and the world.

The world seems to constantly echo with a disconcerting chorus of voices, the result of frustrated relationships between parents and their children, husbands and wives, friends, siblings, in-laws, employees and colleagues — individuals disillusioned with themselves for not being able to relate successfully to their environs. The phenomenal flux of changes in every sphere of our lives since the last century has redefined the role of human relationships. A good relationship today is not one that just lasts but one that coexists with self-respect, individuality and the need to grow.

Everyone's relationship is unique, and people come together for many different reasons. But there are certain things that good relationships have in common such as knowledge, involvement, honest and direct communication, and talking things out quietly. In addition, one should not try too hard to convince the other person of your love, do not question the other person's love all the time, feel the oneness of the universe, step beyond the "me first", do not use your relationships to fulfil your expectations, acknowledge the other person, grow and let grow, check where you went wrong rather than where the other person failed, listen to each other, take the first step in working out a good relationship without worrying about who is right or wrong, know and be yourself. At any stage, it's important that you are always yourself. If you are not yourself, you will feel uncomfortable and would have a very difficult time pretending to be someone that you're not for the entirety of the relationship.

A relationship is normally viewed as a state of relatedness or connection or mutual dealings between people or groups or organizations or societies or countries. From birth to death, success or failure of a person is measured by the kind of relationship he has had with elements of this world: people, nature and beyond it all, with the spirit behind this "relative world". But striking the right chord in a relationship often proves a hard nut to crack.

Relationships are meant to be something different. They are intended, by your source, to be a place in which you extend and receive love, compassion and the joy of taking a life journey together. They are meant to energetically bring you closer such that you share the energies of love, of dreams and of becoming who you next are together. It is meant to give you another, who reflects your energy in so many ways, with whom you can find honesty, with whom you can be reminded of whom you wish to become and with whom you can be corrected by love.

Interpersonal relationships usually involve some degree of interdependence. People in a relationship tend to influence each other, share their thoughts and feelings, and engage in activities together. Because of this interdependence, most things that change or impact one member of the relationship will have some level of impact on the other member.

A strong, healthy relationship can be one of the best supports in your life. Good relationships improve all aspects of your life, strengthening your health, your mind, and your connections with others. However, if the relationship is not working, it can also be a tremendous drain. Relationships are an investment. The more you put in, the more you get back.

# Preface

These tips can help keep a healthy relationship strong, or reinstate trust and love in a relationship on the rocks, and these along with some valuable thoughts and quotes, compiled on Relationship, in this book will provide a helping hand towards you and provide an extra mileage for a happy, meaningful and healthy relationship.

This book incorporates 100 carefully chosen quotations on Relationship, created, modified and mixed. Some of the thoughts presented are ours and the others are from the people who have stood by and worked for the values, some were famous and some were ordinary people. We have acknowledged the persons who have been quoted, wherever we could remember and our sincere thanks are due to all these eminent personalities, who have come up with such inspiring thoughts for this world. Readers are welcome to suggest any amendments and additions.

Ganesha is the God of Wisdom and each of the quotes in this book is accompanied by a painting of Lord Ganesha to inspire you. These paintings have been created by our professional artists keeping in mind the themes of individual quotes.

We prostrate before our parents Smt Kanchan Devi and Shri Bhairav Lal Kogata, and Smt Kamla Devi Nuwal and the late Prof. K.M. Nuwal for their benign blessings that have inspired us to devote ourselves to this cause.

With the expectation of blessings and constructive feedback from all of our esteemed readers,

**Lalita & R.N. Kogata**

Acknowledgement

Quotations from some eminent writers, philosophers and great personalities have been included in this book. Details of the same are given below. We sincerely thank all of them.

| Page no. | Quotation by | Page no. | Quotation by |
|---|---|---|---|
| 15 | Robert Benchley | 68 | Peter Garquharson |
| 22 | Russ Von Hoelscher | 72 | Emily Kimbrough |
| 24 | Brian Tracy | 73 | Dr Jyoce Brother |
| 28 | Stephanie Perkins | 76 | Anthony Robbins |
| 29 | Josh McDowell | 80 | Brian Tracy |
| 35 | Sarah McLachlan | 82 | Stephen R. Covey |
| 36 | Woody Allen | 83 | Linda Festa |
| 37 | Thomas L. Odem, Jr. | 85 | Greg Anderson |
| 38 | Neil LaBute | 88 | Martin Luther |
| 39 | Eric Pepke | 89 | Will Smith |
| 48 | Barbara De Angelis | 91 | Domenico Cieri Estrada |
| 51 | Deepak Chopra | 92 | Franklin D. Roosevelt |
| 53 | Robert Brault | 96 | Leo F. Buscaqlia |
| 54 | Joseph F. Newton | 99 | William Arthur Ward |
| 55 | Max Steingart | 101 | Donald Miller |
| 56 | Wayne Dyer | 104 | Kayal Dawn |
| 60 | Kathryn Hendricks | | |

A good heart and a good nature
are two different qualities.

A good heart
can win many relationships
but a good nature
can win and sustain
life-long relationship.

A lovely relationship should have
the quality of a mirror . . .

which never loses its ability
to reflect even if it is broken
into a thousand pieces.

A true relationship blossoms
when you trust
and respect each other,

and are always honest
whatever be the condition.

Although we have come
to the end of the road,

I still can't let you go,
it's unnatural.

Because . . .
you belong to me
and I belong to you.

Being in a relationship
is not about the kissing,
dating or just showing off.

It's about
being with that person
who makes you happy
in a way no one else can!

Being in a relationship
is a full-time job.

Don't apply
if you aren't ready.

# Being in a relationship:

It's not about the labels
nor about becoming official.

It's about getting to know
someone well enough
to develop genuine and sublime
feelings for that person.

It's about being understanding
and forgiving when
situations are at their worst.

It's about loving someone,
not for what that person
has to offer,
but who and what
the person is.

Compromising
doesn't mean
you are wrong
and someone is right.

It only means
you value your relationship
much more than your ego.

Death ends a life,

not a relationship.

Death is not
the greatest loss in life.

The greatest loss is
when the spirit of relationship
dies within us
while we are still alive!

Distance between two loving hearts
is not an obstacle.

It's a beautiful reminder
of just how strong
a true relationship can be!

Distance doesn't
kill relationship,

Doubts do.

Distance
is not a big factor
in a relationship;
communication is.

But most of all,
commitment is
the biggest factor.

Distance never separates two hearts
that really care,
for our memories span
the miles in seconds
and we are right there.

Distance really doesn't matter
if you truely love the person.

What matters the most is
your honesty and trust
for that relationship to work out.

Do not rush into any kind of relationship.

Work on yourself:
Feel yourself,
Experience yourself
and
Love yourself
for what you are.

Do this first
and you will soon attract
that special loving other.

Each one of us
has the power within
to make others feel
better or worse.

Making others feel better
is much more fun
than making others feel worse.

The former
makes us feel better.

Eighty per cent
of life's satisfaction
comes from
meaningful relationships.

Even the wisest men
make fools of themselves
about women,

and even the most foolish women
are wise enough about men.

Every relationship is
different in content,

so
don't compare
your last one
with the present one.

For a perfect relationship,
it takes:

a lot of practice,
a lot of patience,
a lot of sacrifice,
a lot of love,
a lot of pain,
a lot of regrets,
a lot of honesty
and above all
the truthfulness,

and of course,
a lot of RESPECT.

For the two of us,
home is not just a place.
It is a person.

And WE are finally HOME.

Forgiveness
is
the
oil
of a
lasting relationship.

God,
grant me the serenity
to forget the people
I never liked anyway,

the good fortune
to run into the ones I do,

and the eyesight
to tell the difference.

Good relationship
doesn't need
any promises,
any terms
or conditions.

All it needs is
just two wonderful persons.

GOOD RELATION is:

When someone hurts you,
you don't hurt back.

When someone shouts at you,
you don't shout back.

But when someone needs you,
you always come back.

Good relationships are just like tender saplings.

They demand attention
and care in the beginning,
but once they blossom,
they provide you shade
in all the situations of life.

How lucky I am
to have something
that makes saying
goodbye so hard!

I love you, smile at me,
I love the way your hands reach out
and hold me closer. . . .
This is the heaven to no one else,
other than me.

I think relationship
is like a shark.

It has to keep
moving,
else it dies.

If the essence of my being
has caused a smile
to appear on your face
or a splash of joy
within your heart,

then in living,
I have made my mark.

In a relationship,
you have to open
yourself up,

unwind yourself!

In terms of the formation of
long-term relationships,

it's far better
to get false negatives
than false positives.

In your relationships
with others,
remember the basic and
critically important rule:

If you want to be loved,
be lovable.

It is not important
to go to the heaven
after we leave,

but it is important
to create a heaven
in someone's heart,
before we leave.

Lasting relationship
not only depends
on the spoken words,

but also
on understanding
the unspoken words.

Life is a one-way road,
where you can look back,
but you can't go back.

So, don't miss anything
and enjoy every moment
of life by building trust
in lovely relationship.

Love is not just about hugs, kisses and praises.

It's about trust, compromises, sacrifices and the undying will for the relationship to last.

Love lasts when the ever-lasting relationship comes first.

Lovely times of our life will
not come back
and stay forever.

But the lovely relation and
its mesmerizing memories
will stay in the heart
forever.

Missing someone
gets easier every passing day,
because even though
you are one day further
from the last time
you saw him/her,
you are one day closer
to the next time you will.

More the connections
you and your partner make,
not just the physical,
but between your minds,
your hearts and your souls,

the more you will strengthen
the fabric of your relationship,

the more unforgettable moments
you will experience together.

Most of the relationships fail
not due to the lack of love.

Love is always there . . .

It is just that
one loves too much
and the other one
loves too many.

Never leave a true relationship
for a few faults.

Nobody is born perfect
and nobody is always correct.

At the end,
genuine affection is always
greater than perfection.

No matter, how good or bad
you feel about your relationship,

the person you are with
at the moment
is the right person,

because he or she
reflects your inner self.

No relationship
is actually perfect at all,

unless it consists of two people
who never give up
on each other
despite all hurt or pain.

Once you find someone
to share your ups and downs,

then downs become almost
as good as ups.

People are lonely
because
they build walls
instead of bridges.

Personal relationships
are the fertile soil
from which
all advancement,
all success,
all achievement
in real life
grow.

Problems in
relationship occur
when one is looking
for what is missing
in the other.

Relation
with a good person
is like sugarcane.

You break it,
crush it, squeeze it,
even beat and grind it,

still you always get
only sweetness.

Relationship and medicine play
similar role in our life.

Both relieve us of our pain.

The only difference is
that relationship
has no expiry date.

Relationship
doesn't get closer by meetings,
but it gets sweetened by thoughts.

I care for you
in my own strange ways.

May be you will never know,
may be I will never show.

Relationship
doesn't live in essence,

unless you can
reliably tell the truth
without being prompted.

Relationship is
like a book.

It takes years to write.
But it takes
a few seconds to burn.

So write it carefully.
Protect it, and
don't let it end up
in flames.

Relationship is
like a clear crystal;

you don't realize
how much
you love it
until it breaks.

Relationship
is like a violin.

Music may stop
playing now and then,
but
the strings are attached forever.

So even if you are in touch or not,
you are always remembered.

Relationship is
neither just a meek word,
nor merely a friendship.

It is a
silent commitment,
which says,
I will be with you,
always.

Relationship is not about
finding the right person
but creating the right relation.

It is not how much
you care in the beginning
but how far you care.

Relationship is
not about how long
you have been together,

not how much
you have given or received,

not how many times
you have helped each other.

It is simply how
you value one another.

Relationship
is not holding hands
while you understand
each other.

It's about having
lots of misunderstandings
and still not leaving
each other's hand.

Relationship of trust
depends on our willingness
to look not only after
our own interests,

but also
the interests of others.

Relationships are those:

special moments together,
laughter you have together,
secrets you shared,
promises you made in the heart,
days you waited to meet,
"sorry" you said a million times and,
those stolen smiles and small fights.

Relationships
shouldn't be all about
wanting to change
each other,

but about caring,
loving, sharing,
and honouring
each other's individuality.

Remember!
the best relationship is on
when your love for each other
exceeds the need
for each other.

Remember,
we all stumble . . .
each one of us.

That's why
it's a great comfort
to go hand-in-hand.

Repressed anger can
poison a relationship
as surely as
the cruelest words.

Signs of True Relations:

Speaking without bluffing,
Loving without intentions,
Caring without expectations,
Praying without selfness.

Silence between
two unknown persons
may ignite a relation.

But silence between
two known persons
breaks the relation.

So remain connected.

Some of the biggest challenges in relationships
come from the fact that
most people enter into a relationship
in order to get something.

They're trying to find someone
who's going to make them feel good.

In reality,
the only way a relationship will last is
if you see your relationship
as a place that you are willing to give,
and not as a place
that you are keen to take.

Some relationships
come your way
when you don't need them

and some relationships go
when you realize
you actually need them!

The best relationship
in the world is
when you hold
the hand of a lovely person
and the person
walks along with you
not asking
"where" and "why"?

The best
relationship is

when you relax
side by side
and just talk about
anything
and everything.

The fundamental glue that
holds any relationship
is trust.

The indicator of
true relationship is
openness to tell
everything.

There is no room whatsoever,
for secrets and lies.

The most important ingredient
we put into any relationship
is not what we say
or what we do,
but what we are.

The most important thing
in a relationship
between a man and a woman
is that one of them
must be good
at taking orders.

The most powerful words
in a relationship aren't

"I love you",
"I am with you",
"I will die for you",

it's simply
"I can understand you"!

The relationships
we have with the world
are largely determined by
the relationships
we have with ourselves.

The three things
I want in relationship:

- Eyes that won't cry.
- Lips that won't lie.
- Love that won't die.

The weakest part
of a relationship is
when one of the persons
has to give an explanation
to prove the faith and trust.

Never let it happen!

There is no more satisfying
lovely, friendly, and
charming relationship,
consoling communion,
or company
than
a good marriage.

Throughout the life
people will disrespect you,
treat you bad
and make you mad.

Let God deal with them,
because
hate in your heart
will consume you too.

Time goes by so fast;
people go in and out
of your life.

You should never
miss the opportunity
to tell these people
how much
they mean to you.

To know
when to keep distance
and when to come closer
is the key
to lasting relationship.

Today
we are faced with
the pre-eminent fact that,
if civilization is to survive,
we must cultivate
the science of
human relationships . . .

the ability of all people,
of all kind,
to live together,
in the same world,
at peace.

Trust a person
to the extent that
he feels guilty
to cheat you

and

care for a person
to the extent that
he fears
to lose you.

Value of relationship:

It is not how much
you feel happy
about someone.

But it is how much
someone feels
alone without you.

We are put on earth
not for ourselves,
but for each other.

If you are there
always for others,
then in time of need,
someone will be there
for you.

We need to love others
and to be loved by them.

There is no doubt that
without it, we too,
like an infant left alone,
would cease to grow, cease
to develop,
go mad, and
embrace even death.

We never know

why we like someone
more than others,

why we love someone
without any reason, and

why we feel happy
in their presence.

Certainly, some relationships have
no explanations.

We often don't express
our feelings
due to the fear
of losing a relationship.

But the fact remains,
we lose
a beautiful relationship
just for not expressing
our feelings.

When we seek
to discover the best
in others,

we somehow
bring out the best
in ourselves.

When you are
in a relationship
and it is good,

even if nothing else
in your life is right,

you feel like
your whole world
is complete.

When you stop
expecting people
to be perfect,
you start liking them
for who they are.

Whenever you are
in conflict with someone,
one factor can make the difference
between
damaging your relationship
and deepening it.

That factor is **attitude.**

Why do we say "sorry" even when we're not wrong?
Why do we "bend" ourselves in front of the person we care for?
Why do we feel pleasure in "hurting" the one we love?
Why do we get "consoled" when we cry on the shoulders of those who made us cry?

**Because**

Some pains are more enjoyable than happiness!
Some relations are more important than ego!
Some defeats are more triumphant than victory!
Some moments are more precious than breath!

Without a single thought,
two hands claspe

and

the world finally
makes sense once again.

You can't have
a relationship
without any fights,

but you can make
your relationship
worth a fight.

You hardly pay attention
to a part of your body till
it pains severely.

Don't let it happen
in relationships.